Malaysian Fruits
in Colour

In the jungle of the Tropics I was born,
Wild and untamed, crowned with thorns,
From humble beginnings though I came,
Yet to-day the wide world knows my name.

From a parent towering tall,
Ripenning, to the ground I fall,
In season all my admirers come,
To bid the King of Fruits joyful welcome.

Along crowded streets and in open markets,
My loyal subjects congregate,
Enticed by the nostalgic smell,
Only the defiant do I repel.

On the outside I am thorny and harsh,
In the inside I am soft and lush,
My seeds are covered with tender flesh,
Creamy and aromatic when custard fresh.

Indescribable flavour and vitamins high,
My nourishing value no one can deny,
Once on the palate you will always remember,
Love or hate me now and forever.

Malaysian Fruits in Colour

by

CHIN HOONG FONG

M. AGR. SC., PH. D. (MELB.), M.I. BIOL.

ASSOCIATE PROFESSOR
AGRONOMY AND HORTICULTURE DEPARTMENT
UNIVERSITI PERTANIAN MALAYSIA

and

YONG HOI-SEN

B. SC. PH. D. (MALAYA)

ASSOCIATE PROFESSOR
DEPARTMENT OF GENETICS AND CELLULAR BIOLOGY
UNIVERSITY OF MALAYA

TROPICAL PRESS SDN. BHD.
29 JALAN RIONG
59100 KUALA LUMPUR
MALAYSIA

Copyright © 1980
TROPICAL PRESS SDN. BHD.
29 JALAN RIONG
59100 KUALA LUMPUR
MALAYSIA

First published 1980
Reprinted 1981
Reprinted 1982
Reprinted 1983
Reprinted 1985
Reprinted 1987

ISBN 967-73-0008-3

TYPESETTING, COLOUR SEPARATION,
PRINTED AND BOUND BY ART PRINTING WORKS SDN. BHD.
29 JALAN RIONG, 59100 KUALA LUMPUR
MALAYSIA

Preface

Malaysian fruits in colour is the second of a series of books on the rich flora and fauna of Malaysia. Edible fruits in this country number over a hundred known species. And many more species have yet to be discovered in the jungles. The present collection represents a rich pool of genetic resources, if exploited and strengthened by a strong selection and breeding programme, will no doubt further increase the number of variety of fruits to be found in the local market.

Fruits like papaya, banana and pineapple are available in the market all the year round as there is no fixed season for their production. Unlike the papaya a number of our local fruits appear only twice a year; these are the seasonal fruits like the Durian, Rambutan, Duku, Langsat and many others. Although we have no definite seasons like winter, spring, summer and autumn, we do experience definite hot dry seasons and the wet monsoons. Because different fruits are available at different time of the year, the diversity of local fruits is not fully appreciated or felt by the local populace. In this book an attempt is made to provide information on as many of the fruits grown in this country.

Unlike other Malaysian crops such as padi, oil palm and rubber, fruits are not usually grown in a large commercial scale except the coconut, pineapple and banana. It's only in the last decade that there is commercial interest in fruit cultivation. As an estate crop, these are limited to a few such as durian, rambutan and mangoes. Fruit cultivation is, however, a smallholder's concern, each household growing one or two trees of each species. These are mainly grown for home consumption and excess are sold in the market. With the implementation of the Crop Diversification and Green Book Plan both farmers and home gardeners are encouraged to grow their own fruits. The latest project is the launching of a 3,000 acre orchard in Kedah by FIMA.

It is hoped that this book will be useful to horticulture students, home gardeners, farmers, nurserymen and tourists. Brief descriptions are given on a wide range of fruits, including the local and common names, botanical names and families they belong to. These are illustrated with colour pictures for easy identification which the ordinary black-and-white photos do not permit.

In addition to the description of the various species of fruits found locally, there are three chapters on planting and maintenance of plants, seasonality of fruits and fruit arrangement. The chapter on fruit arrangement illustrates some of the other uses of fruits.

The authors H.F. Chin and H.S. Yong would like to thank the vice chancellors of Universiti Pertanian Malaysia Prof. Tan Sri Mohd. Rashdan bin Hj. Baba and the Vice Chancellor of Universiti Malaya Royal Professor Ungku Aziz for their permission to publish this book.

Contents

Malaysian Fruits in Colour

Common Malaysian Fruits

Malaysia has a rich array of luscious local fruits. The seasonal fruits are generally available in the market about the middle and towards the end and beginning of the year. Unusual weather, however, easily upsets this seasonality.

The common seasonal fruits include the Durian, Rambutan, Mangosteen, Langsat, Duku, Cempedak, Rambai, Bacang, *etc*. Of these, the Durian is the most esteemed and famous of all, regarded by locals and some visitors to be above all other fruits.

There are also many non-seasonal fruits — banana, coconut, a number of citrus, *etc*. Some of these exist in many varieties and fine-flavoured fruits are not uncommon.

In addition to indigenous fruits, non-native species such as the papaya, pineapple, Ciku, guava, pomegranate, water-melon, starfruit, *etc*. also abound in Malaysia. Of these, the papaya, pineapple and water-melon are special favourites and are available all the year round.

Local fruits have been given higher priority status since Malaysia became independent. Every effort indeed has been taken by the Government to encourage the populace to grow and eat more local fruits. With the incentives provided by the Government and the efforts put in by its various agencies such as the Agriculture Department, MARDI and FAMA, there is little doubt that local fruits would have a bright future both within the country as well as overseas.

Durian
Durio zibethinus
BOMBACACEAE

Durian is one of the best known and most controversial of all fruits. It is native to Malaysia and has been cultivated in Tropical Asia for hundreds of years.

The Durian plant is a large and lofty tree some 40 metres tall. The tree may be recognized by the typically bronzy-green, small foliage, and the tall straight trunk topped by almost horizontal branches. During fruiting season, the characteristic olive-green prickly fruit is diagnostic.

Durian fruits vary greatly in size and shape, commonly about 20 cm long by 17.5 cm wide, but may be as large as 35 cm in length. They hang down from the almost horizontal branches on thick stalks, and are covered with coarse, sharp-pointed spines.

The 4–5 segments of the fruit are each filled with 1–7 seeds usually 5–6 cm long by about 1.5 cm wide. Each seed is embedded in a mass of cream or yellow-coloured pulp of a custard-like consistency. It is this pulp which is eaten. It varies a little in its size and colour and much in its flavour. In Peninsular Malaysia, the best durians are held to have a creamy, dark yellow, 'dry' pulp (*durian tembaga*). In Sarawak, the best kinds have a bright orange pulp.

The durian fruit has an extremely high food value. Although the best fruits are

eaten 'raw', they may be eaten with glutinous rice, made into durian cake or preserved with sugar (*lempok*) or salt and prawn paste (*tempoyak*). The unripe fruit is also cooked as vegetable.

Durian trees are generally raised from seeds and buddings. The tree will bear fruit about 7 years old. It takes about 3 months for the fruit to ripen. The two main seasons are between. November to February and from June to August.

Mangosteen, Manggis
Garcinia mangostana
CLUSIACEAE (GUTTIFERAE)

Mangosteen is indigenous to this part of the world. Although it is believed to have been in cultivation for centuries there are no distinct varieties. It is one of the slowest-growing tree and attains about 6–13 metres tall. It takes from seed about 15 years to fruit.

Unlike most other fruits, the cultivated mangosteen reproduces by parthenogenesis, *i.e.* the fruit is produced without fertilization. The fruits are round but slightly flattened at each end. Each fruit has a smooth, thick, firm rind which is pale green at first and ripening to rich purple or red-purple in colour. The apex is crowned with 5–8 flat woody lobes.

A good mangosteen measures some 6–7$\frac{1}{2}$ cm in diameter. Enclosed in the rind are 5–8 fleshy segments which are snowy-white or ivory in colour. The number of

segments corresponds to the number of woody lobes at the apex of the rind. The flavour of the flesh or pulp is slightly acid and delicious.

Mangosteen trees are very commonly grown throughout Malaysia. The fruiting seasons generally follow those of the durian and rambutan.

4

ambutan
ephelium lappaceum
APINDACEAE

The name Rambutan is derived from
e Malay word 'rambut' (meaning
air). Similarly its scientific name
ppaceum in Latin refers to the
esemblance of the fruit to a 'burr'.

The Rambutan fruit is large, oblong or
early round, and measures up to 5–6 cm
ng by 5 cm wide. It is green at the
eginning but ripens to various shades of
d and yellow. Each fruit has a large seed
rrounded with a white or yellowish
ulp (flesh) of varying thickness. The
esh is translucent, firm and juicy but its
avour and quality vary enormously. In
good variety, it is sweet with an
xtremely pleasant, mild, subacid
avour. In the best varieties the flesh
mes away easily from the seed — this is
ferred to as 'Rambutan lekang'.

Rambutan is indigenous to Malaysia
nd has been grown in South-east Asia for
long time. It is a bushy and wide-
owned tree, growing up to 20 metres in
eight. Under suitable conditions the
edling tree fruits at 5 to 6 years.
egetatively-propagated trees (budding
nd marcotting) may start bearing when
to 2 years old. Trees usually fruit twice
year. The main season is between June
nd September.

Pulasan

Nephelium mutabile

SAPINDACEAE

Pulasan, like Rambutan, is indigenous to this part of the world and has been cultivated for many years. Wild trees still exist in the lowland forest. The tree is similar to Rambutan.

The fruits are not very different from Rambutan. They are oblong, measuring 5–6.2 cm by 3.7 cm. The skin is dark red when ripe and is covered with short, thick and fleshy spines. The flesh is translucent, usually whitish and tastes quite sweet. Several races are grown and these differ in quality of fruit. The fruiting season of Pulasan is similar to the Rambutan.

Mata Kucing
Euphoria malaiense
SAPINDACEAE

The name Mata Kucing literally translated means Cat's Eye. The Chinese, however, calls it Dragon's Eye (from Longan, a name given to the related Chinese fruit not found in this country).

Mata kucing is also native to this part of the world and wild trees are found in the forests. The tree has an attractive shape and may attain a height of 20 metres.

The fruits are round, up to 2 cm in diameter. The pale brownish skin is rough and tough. The flesh is translucent, whitish and sweet. The amount of flesh varies a great deal; in very good variety it may be 0.5 cm thick. Unlike Rambutan and Pulasan, the seeds are extremely large in relation to the amount of flesh.

Indian mango, Mangga
Mangifera indica
ANACARDIACEAE

The Indian Mango is the typical mango fruit. It was known to the people of India since the days of antiquity and

has been cultivated by Man for over 4,000 years. This is the commonest and most variable mango in Malaysia. The tree grows up to 27 metres tall.

The fruits are slightly beaked at one side. They vary enormously in size and shape. The colour of the skin when ripe is as variable — green, yellow or orange. Similarly the flowers may be greenish yellow, white, pale cream or even pinkish.

The ripe mango fruit is eaten as dessert. The flesh is bright yellow, and in good varieties very juicy and sweet, and at times aromatic. Unripe fruit is also eaten raw and may be quite sour. The fruit is rich in vitamins A and C and has been demonstrated to have better food value than the apple.

Many varieties of Indian Mango are found in Malaysia. The good exotic varieties include the Apple Mango, Mulgoa, Harumanis, Thai Mango, Indian Papaya Mango, Philippines Mango, Taiwan Mini Apple Mango, Indian Coconut Mango, *etc.* The local varieties are generally regarded as inferior in flavour.

Most existing trees in this country are grown from seedlings but vegetative methods (especially grafting) are now widely practised particularly on the imported varieties. The trees usually flower and fruit after the fourth year. Some grafts, however, may begin to bear a few flowering shoots in the second year after planting. Flowering is usually not regular. The quality of the fruit is also dependent on the prevailing climate. It does best when there is a definite dry spell and little rain at flowering and fruiting time.

Horse-Mango, Bacang
Mangifera foetida
ANACARDIACEAE

Bacang is an indigenous Malaysian fruit. It grows to about 20–27 metres high. It can be distinguished from other mangoes by its scentless, pinkish red flowers borne on copper red flower stalks. Flowers are produced almost throughout the year in different localities, but mainly in two flushes once about December to March and the other about May to July.

The fruits are oval in shape, measuring 8.5–13.5 cm long by 5–10 cm wide. Although quite inedible when immature because of the occurrence of a poisonous sap, the fruits are much eaten when ripe. The skin of the fruit is smooth, dull and green to yellowish green scattered with minute dark dots. The flesh is fibrous and orange or yellow in colour; the pale yellow varieties are said to be sweeter and less fibrous with less smell (that of turpentine). The fruits are also used in curries for making chutney, for pickles, and sometimes made into sweetmeats.

Kuini
Mangifera odorata
ANACARDIACEAE

Kuini is a native Malaysian fruit. It grows to about 20–27 metres in height.

Unlike Bacang (*Mangifera foetida*), Kuini fruits are described by most authors as having a fragrant smell or "a strong smell, but not unpleasantly so"; some even describe it as reminiscent of durians. The oblong fruits, up to 12.5 by 10 cm, are very similar to the Bacang except that they usually do not have an obvious point to one side and the flesh has a light orange colour and is juicy sweet. Indeed Kuini has been regarded by some as a variety of Bacang. Unlike Bacang, Kuini flowers are strongly fragrant — the pink flowers are borne on yellowish or reddish brown panicles. The trees flower throughout the year. Like Bacang, immature Kuini fruits contain a poisonous sap. The fruits are also used in curries, for making chutney and for pickles.

Papaya, Betik
Carica papaya
CARICACEAE

Papaya is a sappy, soft-tissued, quic
growing but short-lived plant. It grows
2–10 metres in height. It is believed to h

native of tropical America, where it is called pawpaw as well as *melon zapote*. Today, it is grown in tropical countries situated between latitudes 32°N and °S. All parts of the plant produce a milky juice (or latex), which contains the enzymes papain and chymopapain, both of which have protein-digesting and milk-clotting properties.

The plants are usually dioecious (only male or female flowers are present). Male and female plants are identical in appearance until flowers appear. They come into bearing at about 6–12 months. The fruits vary greatly in size, shape and flavour. They may measure 7–60 cm long and weighing up to 9 kg. They are usually eaten when ripe as dessert. The flesh is very rich in vitamin A and calcium and has also some vitamin C.

Many varieties of papaya are grown in Malaysia. Among the better known ones,

the yellow-fleshed type includes Serdang, Honey Dew, and Morib, while the red-fleshed kind includes Batu Arang, Subang 6 and Taiping 3.

Banana, Pisang

Musa

MUSACEAE

The banana is one of the most ancient food plants, having been used, and perhaps cultivated, at the dawn of recorded history. It is grown between °N and S of the Equator. It is a perennial herb with a height of 2–9 etres. The time to shooting is 7–9 onths, and the time from shooting to arvesting is about 90 days.

The fruit is a berry. The individual uits are sometimes called 'fingers', each uster of friuts is called a 'hand' and the uit bunch is called a 'stem'. A bunch of anana may contain 5–15 hands with -20 fingers each.

The size, shape, skin colour, and the avour, texture and colour of the flesh ary with the cultivars (or vatieties). Many varieties are grown in Malaysia. hey may be grouped into two ategories: those which are eaten raw ecause of their fine flavour (*e.g.* Pisang mbun or Jamaican banana, Pisang Mas, Pisang Rastali, *etc.*), and those which are cooked before eating (*e.g.* Pisang Abu or Ashy Plantain, Pisang

Awak, Pisang Tandok, *etc.*).

The banana is nutritionally similar to potato; the calorific value being about 100 calories per 100 grams. It has also a good content of vitamin A and fair in vitamin C.

Coconut, Kelapa, Nyiur
Cocos nucifera
PALMAE

Coconut palms are trees of the tropic coastlands. It is believed that the cocon tree originated in the tropical coas possibly those of Malaysia.

There are a large number of varieties coconut palm, differing either in the n or stature. They may, however, l grouped into two main types according stature — dwarfs and talls. The ta variety grows to a height of 30 metres more. It takes about 5 or 6 years mature and then yields continuously fo many years, reaching its best about i 30th year. In contrast, the dwarf varie begins to fruit one year earlier an reaching its prime towards its 15th yea It also produces more nuts but its lif span is shorter.

The more or less oval nuts are borne the base of the fronds. They take about months to attain full size, after which th shell hardens and the flesh (meat endosperm) begins to form. By the tim the nuts ripen they are about a year ol

The main commercial product coconut is its copra, the dried flesh of th nut. Most of the copra is processed for o locally and is used in the making cooking oil, margarine, soap, candles, *et*

As food, the nuts are used fresh i

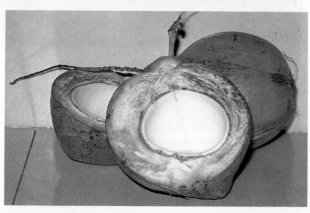

cooking or dessicated for confectionery and cakes. 'Santan', the coconut milk produced by grating the meat, has been and still is an important culinary ingredient among Malaysians. Immature full-sized nuts are also becoming increasingly popular as a source of refreshing drink.

A brown sugar known as 'Gula Melaka' or 'Gula Kelapa' is made from the sap or juice of the immature inflorescence. The immature inflorescence is also tapped to produce a palm wine called toddy.

Pineapple, Nanas
Ananas comosus
BROMELIACEAE

The native home of the pineapple is eastern South America. The Malaysian name *nanas* and the scientific name *Ananas* as well as other names are derived from the Tupi Indian name *Nana*.

The pineapple is a collective fruit, *i.e.* it develops from a whole inflorescence with

many flowers and not from a single flower as for example in durians.

In cultivation, good varieties of pineapple seldom produce seeds, hence they are propagated vegetatively. Such reproduction also ensures uniformity of the variety. The seeds, when formed, are normally used for the production of new variety.

There are many cultivated varieties of pineapple. The most important commercial varieties in Malaysia fall into two groups — those for canning (Nanas Merah and Nanas Hijau) and those for eating raw (Nanas Sarawak and Nanas Moris). The fruits of Nanas Sarawak are medium-sized with pale yellow flesh and thick central woody core. Those of Nanas Moris are small, with fairly bright yellow flesh and thin central woody core. They are usually very sweet and perhaps the best for dessert.

The fruit also forms one of the main ingredients of a local salad preparation called *rojak*. It also makes excellent jam.

Water Melon, Tembikai
Citrullus lanatus
CUCURBITACEAE

The water melon is a native of tropical and subtropical Africa but has been cultivated since ancient times. Unlike other fruits, water-melon plants have weak, creeping stems and climb by tendrils, and the fruit ripen on the ground.

The fruits vary greatly in size and shape; colour, texture and thickness of the skin; colour, texture, flavour and sugar content of flesh; and colour, size and number of seeds. Many varieties are available in Malaysia. The plants are grown from seeds. The fruits are ready for harvesting about 100 days or more after sowing.

The water-melon fruit is usually eaten raw as a favourite thirst quencher. In addition to the flesh, dried parched seeds called 'kuaci' are also consumed.

Sapodilla, Ciku

Manilkara achras
SAPOTACEAE

The Ciku is a small evergreen fruit tree, native to Southern Mexico, Guatemala and Honduras. The trees are propagated by marcotting and inarching, in addition to growing from seeds. They begin to fruit about 3–4 years after planting.

Fruits are produced at frequent intervals throughout the year. They take about 4 months to mature from flowering. They are round or oval in shape, measuring about 5–10 cm long and weighing about 113 g. Mature fruits have a dull, rather mealy, pale to rusty, brown, and thin skin. The flesh, when ripe, is soft and pulpy, granulated and yellowish to pinkish brown in colour.

Unripe fruits are unpleasantly astringent. Ripe fruits, however, are much appreciated by many people as a dessert fruit. The flesh has been likened to that of a pear.

Jackfruit, Nangka
Artocarpus heterophyllus
MORACEAE

Jackfruit is probably native to India. As it is usually grown from seed there is considerable variation between trees, particularly in the shape, size and quality of the fruits. The tree grows up to 20 metres tall. It is quick-growing and may bear fruit when about 3 years old.

The fruit is a gigantic syncarp (a compound fruit) measuring 30–90 cm by 25–50 cm, and is the largest of all cultivated fruits. It is barrel- or pear-shaped. The rind is pale to dark yellow and is completely covered with short sharp hexagonal fleshy spines. The flesh is golden yellow and waxy while the seeds are large (3 × 2 cm) with thick gelatinous brown covering. In between the seeds are soft fleshy fibres which are the unfertilized flowers.

Ripe Jackfruit has a strong, rather Durian-like smell. It forms an important source of food — the edible flesh contains

23.4% carbohydrates while the seed has 38.4%. There is also a fair amount of protein in the seed (6.6%). The seed is eaten when cooked.

There are very few varieties of Jackfruit in Malaysia. These may be grouped into two kinds — those with soft flesh around the seeds and those with firm flesh.

Cempedak
Artocarpus integer
MORACEAE

Cempedak is a native to this part of the world. Indeed wild Cempedak is found scattered in the high forest throughout the mainland from the lowlands to an altitude of 1300 metres. Like Nangka, the tree grows up to 20 metres tall but bears fruit about 5 years after germination.

Cempedak fruit is also a collective or compound fruit. It is borne on the trunk or main branches and attains a dimension of 20–50 cm by 10–15 cm. The rind is golden yellow to light brown, covered with numerous fleshy spines. The flesh is golden yellow to light brown, with a rather slimy, custard-like texture. It is eaten raw or deep fried together with the seed. Its flavour is very strong, reminescent of Durian and Bacang. Its food value is similar to Nangka.

Breadfruit, Breadnut, Sukun
Artocarpus altilis
MORACEAE

The breadfruit is a native of Polynesia where it is an important staple food. It was the centre of some romantic history (Mutiny on the Bounty, 1787) in the 18th century. Although it has been introduced into most tropical countries, it has not attained much importance except in the West Indies.

Like Nangka and Cempedak, the breadfruit is formed from the whole inflorescence. It is more or less round, measuring 10–30 cm in diameter. Two forms of fruits — seedless and seeded — are to be found. They are used more as a vegetable than as a fruit. The seedless varieties may be sliced, boiled or baked whole, or ground up and made into biscuits. The edible portion, which constitutes about 70% of the fruit, is made up of about 20% carbohydrates. In the seeded forms (known as breadnut), the seeds are eaten after cooking and have a chestnut flavour.

Sentul, Kecapi
Sandoricum koetjape
MELIACEAE

Sentul is native to Malaysia. It is cultivated throughout the country. There are two distinct forms — Yellow (Yellow Sentul) and Red (Kecapi). The tree grows to about 50 metres in height.

The fruits are more or less round, about —7.5 cm in diameter. They have a thick, irm and velvety rind, which varies in colour from dull yellow to golden yellow and sometimes flushed with pink. The pulp is white, translucent and juicy. The flavour is pleasant and in some the ripe fruit smells like ripe peaches.

Langsat and Duku
Lansium domesticum
MELIACEAE

Both Langsat and Duku are native to this part of the world, but have been in cultivation for a very long time. Although their fruits can be readily distinguished, they are regarded as belonging to the same species, namely *Lansium domesticum*. The trees grow to about 8–17 metres tall.

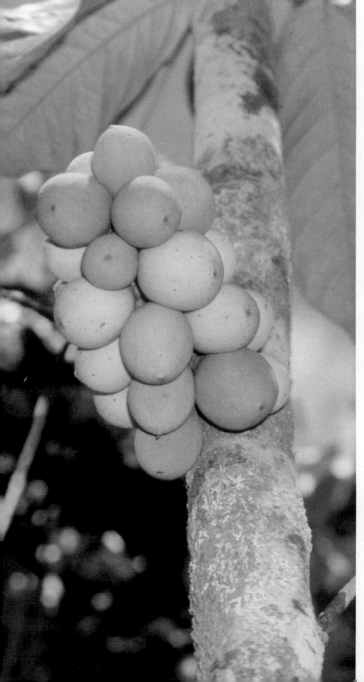

Ripe Langsat fruits have thin skin with milky juice and are oval in shape and measure up to 3.7 cm wide. In contrast ripe Duku fruits have thick skin without milky juice and are round in shape measuring 5 cm wide. Furthermore Langsat has commonly about 20 fruits on the main stalk while Duku has about 8–12 fruits.

The flesh in both Langsat and Duku is usually white in colour; pink-fleshed forms also occur in Duku. It is juicy but the flavour, although always refreshing, varies from sweet to sour. Each fruit is made up of 5 unequal-sized segments, some of which may contain a large, thick seed that tastes very bitter.

In Peninsular Malaysia, Langsat is frequently cultivated in the north while Duku appears mainly in the south. There are also other forms of Langsat known as Duku-Langsat in Trengganu and the Kelantan Duku.

Both Langsat and Duku are slow growing, taking from seed about 15 years to bear fruit. They usually bear twice a year, about the middle of the year and the end-and-beginning of the year.

Rambai

Baccaurea motleyana

EUPHORBIACEAE

Rambai is native to Malaysia and Sumatra and is commonly grown in Malaysian village gardens. The tree is densely leafy and heavy looking, reaching up to some 20 metres tall.

The fruits hang in communal strings (racemes) from the twigs, main branches and to a lesser extent, from the upper part of the trunk. Each fruit measures about 2–4 cm, usually slightly longer than wide. It is buff-coloured and has a smooth and thin skin.

Within each fruit occurs a variable number of seeds enclosed in a translucent white pulp. The seeds are comparatively large and the pulp varies considerably in its quality, from rather acid to sweet and palatable. Rambai season generally follows that of the durians around August–September.

Malay Apple, Pomerac, Jambu Merah

Eugenia malaccensis
(syn. *Syzygium malaccensis*)

MYRTACEAE

Malay Apple is a native of Malaysia. The tree grows up to 20 metres high. It is often planted as an ornamental or windbreak. It has very striking flowers which are vivid crimson-pink and measure 5–7.5 cm in diameter. The fruits are oblong or pyriform, about 5–7.5 cm by 6.2 cm when ripe and are reddish pink or white striped crimson-pink. The flesh is rather dry but quite pleasant to eat.

Water Apple, Jambu Air
Eugenia aquea
(syn. *Syzygium aqueum*)
MYRTACEAE

Water Apple is a native of India a has been in cultivation for ma centuries. The tree grows to 5–8 met high.

Flowers are slightly scented, about 2 cm wide, white or occasionally pinki The fruits have an uneven shape, with wide apex and a narrow base. They m be white to bright pink in colour. T pulp is crisp and watery, with a scent flavour, hence the name watery ro apple. The flesh may also be insipid. T skin contains a high content of vitamin In Malaysia the fruits are eaten mainly children although they are good thi quenchers.

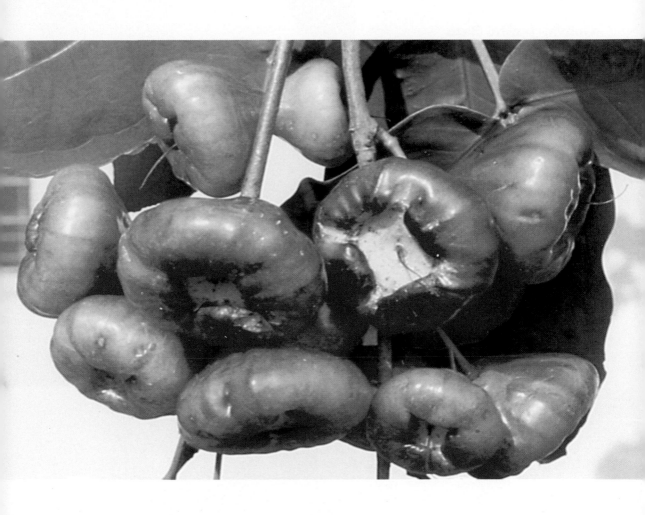

Guava, Jambu Batu

Psidium guajava

MYRTACEAE

Guava is indigenous to tropical America but has been naturalized in many countries including Malaysia. The tree grows to about 8 metres high, with characteristic smooth, pale mottled bark that peels off in thin flakes.

The fruits are very variable in size, shape and flavour but all have a strong sweet smell. Those of good varieties are sweet while others may be tart. In Malaysia, ripe juicy sweet types are eaten fresh, particularly the recently introduced seedless variety, or made into juice. The two common forms are yellow or pink-fleshed.

Guava fruit is a rich source of vitamin C. It has been estimated to contain 2–5 times the vitamin C content of fresh orange juice.

Rose Apple, Jambu Mawar
Eugenia jambos
(syn. *Syzygium jambos*)
MYRTACEAE

Rose Apple is native to the Indo-Malaysian region and has been cultivated for centuries. The tree grows up to 10 metres in height. The fruits are ovoid shaped, about 4 cm in diameter. When ripe they may be greenish or whitish tinged yellow or pink. The flesh is whitish and rose-scented. It may be eaten fresh or made into preserves. Fruits of poor quality may be dry and tasteless.

Pomegranate, Delima
Punica granatum
LYTHRACEAE

The pomegranate originated from Persia. It does not grow very well in this country. It is a weak shrub with sparse foliage growing to a height of 3–4 metres. It can also be planted in pots, as some people are satisfied just to have only the flowers which are fairly large and attractive, bright orange in colour. The fruits are found at the end of twigs or branches which usually droop as the fruits are heavy and the branches weak. Each fruit may, under local conditions, grow to 10–12.5 cm in diameter. It has a smooth shiny skin, greenish with a tinge of red when young but turning brownish yellow or reddish when ripe. The tip of the fruit is crowned with the remains of the sepals.

Each fruit is divided into about half a dozen compartments. Each compartment contains many small seeds surrounded by shiny pinkish red flesh which is full of juice. The seeds are packed tightly together. It is difficult to eat this fruit as each seed has to be taken out slowly and there is not much to eat. Although this species has been introduced for a long time, it is not very widely grown.

Passion fruit, Buah Susu
Passiflora edulis
PASSIFLORACEAE

The passion fruits are of tropical origin from South America. They are named after the Passion flower. There are a few species; this particular one is distinguished by the greenish yellow fruits and belongs to the same species as the purple-fruit variety found in the highlands. The plants are climbers with the aid of tendrils, and coil round supports such as fences or pergola.

The flowers are typical of the passion flower with prominent outgrowth from the petals (corona). The fruits are egg shaped about 5–10 cm long and 7.5 cm across. They are green when immature, turning yellow on ripening. The skin is smooth shiny and fairly hard. The rind is about 1/8 inch thick; inside are numerous black seeds covered with orange yellow pulp. The fruits can be eaten fresh or made into juice, ice cream or cake.

In the home garden passion fruit can be grown along fences. The plants are propagated from cuttings or seeds.

Great Hog Plum, Kedondong
Spondias cytherea
ANACARDIACEAE

Kedondong belongs to the same family as the mangoes. It is introduced from the Pacific Islands. It is fairly common but grown mainly as individual tree in the rural areas. It grows rapidly to a height of 10–20 metres, and fruits all the year round.

The flowers are tiny and greenish white in colour, grouped together as a panicle. The fruits are bright green, on ripening turning yellowish with a lot of greyish brown freckles. Each fruit is about 7.5–10 cm long by 2.5–3.7 cm wide. It is eaten as a fresh fruit or pickled. The flesh is white and crunchy when immature, becomes fibrous on ripening. Inside each fruit is a large fibrous seed. The plant is propagated from seeds.

Palmyra Palm, Sea Apple, Lontar
Borassus flabellifera
PALMAE

Lontar belongs to the same family as the coconut. This species is of Asian origin and well known for its varied uses in that every part of the palm is useful. In Malaysia, it is found mainly in the northern part. It is not a very tall palm growing to 10–13 metres tall. Is has a beautiful crown of large palmate leaves.

The fruits are borne in bunches like the coconuts but they are much smaller and rounded; each measures about 10–12.5 cm in diameter and is slightly flattened at both ends. They are colourful, with dark purple skin and a set of green bracts at the base. Unlike the coconut, each fruit has 3 seeds; the fleshy part of each seed resembles the meat of the coconut and there is present also small quantity of water. Both the flesh and water are edible and eaten fresh or made into an ice drink.

41

Nutmeg, Buah Pala
Myristica fragrans
MYRISTICACEAE

Nutmeg has its origin in Eastern Malaysia but had spread to India and Europe centuries ago. Although it is well known as spice and dried fruits, one does not see the fresh fruit in the market.

The tree is usually small but has the capacity to grow up to about 23 metres. It has male and female plants but bisexual ones also occur. The male tree is essential for proper fertilization. Fruits are found in female and hermaphrodite or bisexual trees. The fruit is heart-shaped, about 7.5 cm long and 5 cm wide. The fruit is green turning to yellow brown on ripening. When it is ripe it splits into two halves, inside of which is a large brown seed covered with the coral red mace. It is seldom eaten raw.

Nutmeg has many uses — medicinal, spice, sweets, pickles and oil. It is not found in home gardens and is grown mainly in Penang on a small scale.

Malay Gooseberry, Cermai
Cicca acida

EUPHORBIACEAE

The Malay Gooseberry is rarely found in the market except in odd kampongs. It is grown in limited areas, mainly in the northern states. The tree resembles that of Blimbing Asam. It flowers all the year round. The roundish fruits, of pale yellow green colour, are very attractive. The surface is smooth but slightly ridged, while the base and apex are flattened. The fruit when ripe is yellowish white in colour. There is a small angular hard seed at the centre of the fruit. The fruit is eaten fresh but is best used as a pickle as it is very sour.

Pomelo, Limau Betawi
Citrus grandis
RUTACEAE

Pomelo is the biggest of all citrus fruits; each fruit weighing from 0.5–1.4 kg. It is cultivated all over Malaysia and fruits all the year round. Pomelo trees are evergreen and grow to a height of 10 metres. The fruit is round with flattened tip. Its size varies from 12.5 to 25 cm across. The rough outer skin is light green to yellowish in colour while the inner skin is white to pinkish and spongy. The thickness of the skin varies from 0.6 to 2.5 cm. The edible part of the fruit is made up of 10–15 segments. It is juicy but may be sweet or sour. Two main forms with pale cream or pinkish colour are found. The seeds are about 1.2 cm long.

Pomelo is a popular fruit, appearing specially at Chinese festive seasons. It can be propagated by seeds, marcotting or grafting. The Tambun fruits from Perak are famous throughout Malaysia.

Musk Lime, Limau Kesturi
Citrus microcarpa
RUTACEAE

This is a common plant in the home garden, either as a potted plant or planted in the garden. It grows to about 3–4 metres tall. The fruits are very small compared to other citrus. It is roundish (about 2.5–3.7 cm across) with a smooth, shiny, thin skin. The skin is often made rough and warty by insect damage. Immature fruits are green but turn yellow or orangy when ripe. Inside each fruit are 6–8 segments which often contain seeds. They are very juicy but sour, hence not eaten as dessert but rather as a refreshing fruit juice. They are also commonly pickled with salt, and can also be preserved with sugar as dried fruits.

The plant fruits all the year round and can be easily propagated by marcotting as well as from seeds.

Common Lime, Limau Asam, Limau Nipis
Citrus aurantifolia
RUTACEAE

The common lime is another popular fruit. It grows to about 5 metres tall. In the early years, it is a thorny shrub. The fruits are roundish, about 2.5–5 cm in diameter, green when immature but turning yellow at maturity. The skin is shiny and smooth, about 0.3–1.2 cm thick. Each fruit has about a dozen segments with seeds embedded within each. The segments are greenish yellow in colour and are very juicy but sour, hence normally not eaten as dessert but as a fruit juice.

The common lime is really common and can be found throughout the country, in markets, coffee shops, and in many home gardens. It is easily grown from seeds but most commonly propagated by marcots.

Sweet Orange, Limau Manis
Citrus suhuiensis
RUTACEAE

Oranges here, in general, do not grow as well as those of the temperate zones. They are very variable in quality. Limau Manis is greenish to yellow in colour, and does not resemble the true oranges. It is not commonly grown except in some localized areas like Perak.

The fruits are rounded in shape, growing to 5–10 cm in diameter. The skin is shiny and green or greenish yellow, and it can be peeled off easily. Each fruit has 10–15 segments. The flesh is yellowish to orangy, very juicy, and tastes sourish to sweet. Each segment may contain one or several seeds.

This variety of oranges is of limited use, mainly as a dessert fruit. It fruits all the year round and can be propagated easily by marcotting or sometimes from seeds.

Mandarin Orange, Tangerine, Limau Cina, Limau Manis
Citrus nobilis

RUTACEAE

Mandarin oranges have been cultivated for thousands of years. Malaysia imports tons of them annually during the Chinese New Year. They are grown in a small scale in Cameron Highlands where they are capable of producing nice big fruits.

The fruit varies in size between varieties, generally 7.5–12.5 cm diameter and flattened at both ends. It is rough outside with orange or yellow orange, shiny soft skin which can be peeled off very easily. Each fruit has 10–15 segments which are very juicy and sweet.

Lemon, Limau
Citrus limon
RUTACEAE

Lemon is found originally in Asia and introduced to other parts of the world. It grows to 3–4 metres tall. It is not as common as Limau Nipis or Kesturi, but occurs in different parts of the country.

The fruits are green turning to yellow on ripening. They are longish, about 7.5–12.5 cm by 5–7.5 cm, and may be pointed or blunt at the tip.

Lemon fruit juice is refreshing and nutritious. The plant can be easily propagated by marcotting or from seeds.

Wild Lime, Limau Purut
Citrus hystrix
RUTACEAE

Limau Purut has outstanding characters which differ from the general group of oranges and lemons. It is a small tree 3–5 metres tall. The fruit is pear-shaped, about 10 cm by 5–7.5 cm, dark green turning yellow on ripening, and very wrinkled and rough. The fruit is not eaten as a fresh dessert fruit as juice is lacking. It is mainly used as a flavouring in food. It may also be used as a hair shampoo.

The leaves, about 7.5–10 cm long, are used as a spice in curries.

Limau Purut can be planted in big pot as an ornamental. It is propagated from seeds or marcots.

Carambola, Starfruit, Blimbing Manis
Averrhoa carambola
OXALIDACEAE

This is a popular fruit tree of the orient. It grows up to 10 metres high with many branches. The leaves are compound in nature, *i.e.* each consists of 2 to 5 pairs of leaflets, which are rounded at the base and pointed at the tip.

Flowers are produced in panicles on the twigs by the leaves all the year round.

The tiny lilac flowers are beautiful. The fruits are deeply ridged; a cross section is star-shaped hence the common name starfruit. The length of the fruit varies from 5 to 17.5 cm. The surface is smooth, shiny, and waxy. Immature fruits are green, turning yellow or orange at maturity. The yellow flesh is usually soft and juicy and tastes from sour to very sweet. Seeds are flat and often embedded in the centre. The fruits can be put to various uses; the sweet varieties are for dessert, the sour ones for jelly, jam and juice. They are rich in vitamin C.

Lately starfruits are produced more abundantly in tin tailings. These areas with well drained soil and added high organic fertilizers are very suitable for their growth. In Malaysia they are quite common in kampong gardens and backyards. They are readily propagated by seeds but will not be true to type, therefore budding is usually carried out to maintain quality. No known horticultural varieties have been named but those grown around Sungai Besi and Serdang in the State of Selangor are famous for their quality. There are distinct differences in their quality, flavour and colour.

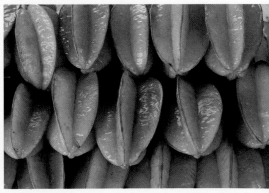

Blimbing Asam; Belimbing Buluh, Bilimbi
Averrhoa bilimbi
OXALIDACEAE

A native of Malaysia, it usually grows into a small slender tree up to 10 metres tall. It is quite commonly grown in the kampongs. Blimbing Asam can be easily distinguished from the starfruit in that it has large leaves with 10–34 leaflets. The leaves are paler green than the starfruit. Flowers are produced all the year round especially during the drier parts of the year. The crimson flowers are borne on the stem and branches. Fruits are cylindrical or slightly 5 angled in shape and vary from 5–10 cm long. They are greenish yellow to yellow when ripe, and are soft and fleshy with a few flat seeds in the centre. They are juicy but very sour, and are eaten as pickles or cooked as seasonings or curries. It is also possible to make candies and jams out of them.

Soursop, Durian Blanda
Annona muricata
ANNONACEAE

It is a small slender evergreen tree growing to a height of about 7 metres. It thrives best in the tropical lowlands with rich deep loam. Of the three Annonas, this is the easiest to grow (without much cultural requirements), and has prolific fruiting capacities. The soursop fruit is the largest among the Annonas, weighing around 1 kg or more. It is long, heart shaped, dark green in colour with short fleshy spines. The flesh or pulp is white, soft, juicy and fragrant. In between the pulp are embedded brown to blackish seeds. The fruit can be eaten as a dessert fruit. As it is rather fibrous, it is often made into a drink *i.e.* extract of juice from pulp.

Soursop is a common local fruit with a good potential for the canning industry as a good flavour nutritious drink. It is quite easily grown from seed, marcotting and budding. Its quality can be improved by breeding and selection or by improved cultural methods, making it a profitable crop of commercial importance as well as a backyard plant in the home garden.

Sugar Apple, Sweet Sop, Seri Kaya, Buah Nona,

Annona squamosa

ANNONACEAE

This species is from South America; different names have been given to it depending on the place where it was introduced. In Malaysia it is popularly known as Seri Kaya.

The small tree grows to a height of about 5 metres. Flowers are usually produced singly but at times in groups of 2 or 3. A fully grown fruit is a rounded heart shaped structure about 5–10 cm in diameter. It is yellowish green when ripe. The surface is rough and tuberculate. The fleshy pulp is whitish in colour, sweet and slightly acidic. It is not juicy, therefore eaten mainly as a dessert fruit. Each of the carpels has a brownish seed like a pointed bean.

Seri Kaya or sweet sop is widely grown in Malaysia. It grows best in rich deep soil and needs constant manuring. The plants can be grown from seeds or best propagated by air layering or marcotting so as to produce plants which are true to type.

Custard Apple, Bullock's Heart, Nona Kapri, Nona

Annona reticulata

ANNONACEAE

This is the least popular or well known of the Annonas in Malaysia. It came from the West Indies and South America. The tree is slightly taller than that of Seri Kaya and grows to a height of 7–8 metres. It sometimes shed its leaves, behaving as semi-deciduous. Flowers are often produced in clusters. The mature fruit is heart shaped, sometimes oval or conical. It is slightly larger than the Seri Kaya, weighing from 0.1–1.2 kg. It takes a long time to mature. The surface of the fruit is smooth with hexagonal lines and reddish brown in colour. The flesh, like the other Annonas, is pulpy and contains numerous brown seeds. The fruit does not taste as good as the others, lacking flavour, thus not as popular.

Fruit Scene Market Place.

Rare Fruits

The term rare in this context refers to fruits which are very rarely seen in the market or grown locally *i.e.* they are uncommon or infrequently available in the main market, to the majority of the population. The reasons for this rarity may be that they are difficult to grow, or they are not popular because of their taste, smell or of poor storability. Lastly they are eaten only in certain parts of the country, for example many of the fruits grown in the East Coast of Peninsular Malaysia are not available in other parts of the country.

In addition to the species described here there are other fruits described in this book which may be also classified as rare. In the case of Sapucaia nut, not many Malaysians have tasted or even heard of it. It is indeed a rare fruit but as it fits in better in the chapter on nuts, it is not included here.

Kerandang, Karaunda

Carissa congesta

APOCYNACEAE

This is a small tree, 3–5 metres tall, belonging to the same family as Frangipani. It is a native of India but is cultivated locally mainly in villages for fruits and in some gardens as ornamental. It is a beautiful tree when it is full bearing but it is rather thorny and prickly, and produces latex.

This small tree produces small whitish flowers measuring 3.5 cm across. The fruits are pinkish white, very sour and therefore used mainly as pickles but can also be made into jam or cooked.

Avocado pear, Apukado

Persea americana

LAURACEAE

Avocado pear is a native of Mexico, spreading to other tropical regions. It is an evergreen tree but some varieties do shed their leaves. It grows to 10–20 metres tall, with an erect stem and spreading branches. There are many varieties of Avocados, a few are doing well in Serdang.

The time of flowering varies between varieties and location. Large number of flowers are produced at the ends of branches. They are rather small, yellowish green in colour. The fruit is also very variable in shape, from 'typical' pear shape to cucumber-like. Each fruit may weigh up to 1 kilogram. The colour is yellowish green when young but on ripening changes to maroon, purple or even black. The skin is rather thin while the flesh is thick and greenish yellow in colour. The fruit is very rich in oil and minerals and has a nutty flavour. It is not sweet but may be eaten with salt and pepper, or as a dessert or even soup.

Avocado grows well in well drained soil with regular manuring. It is quite a hardy plant, and does not seem to be attacked by pests. Because of its high food value, this crop should be more widely grown, but suitable varieties have to be found for the local climate. When grown from seeds, it takes 6 years to bear fruit of uncertain quality. The best method of propagation is by budding.

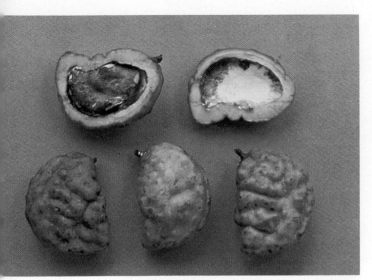

Nam-Nam

Cynometra cauliflora

FABACEAE (LEGUMINOSAE)

This tree belongs to the bean family. It is a small tree with a thick much branched stem. Each leaf is made up of 2 leaflets, which if not examined closely may appear as 2 leaves. The leaflet is asymmetrical in shape measuring 5–15 cm long and 2.5–7.5 cm wide. It is shiny smooth, dark green above and paler below.

The flowers are rather small about 1.2 cm across. They appear on the stem in clusters. The fruits are kidney-shaped, 5–10 cm long and 5 cm wide. The pod does not split open readily, but a line is visible along the fruit and divides it into two. The texture of the fruit surface is rough and wrinkled, pale greenish/yellow and dull looking. The flesh is juicy and yellow in colour. It produces a smell and tastes sourish. The seeds are large.

Nam-nam is a native of Malaysia grown mainly in northern Peninsular Malaysia and can be more widely cultivated in other states, mainly in kampongs and villages.

Butterfruit, Buah Mentaga
Diospyros discolor
EBENACEAE

This plant belongs to a family which is well known for its wood *i.e.* ebony which is mainly used for art and not for construction of buildings. This species, native of the Philippines, can grow to a big tree of 20 metres or more but locally usually small trees are produced. Its habit is a small spreading tree with drooping branches. The leaves are smooth but covered with soft fine hairs. They are fairly large, 7.5–22.5 cm long by 2.5–7.5 cm wide. The leaves are dark green on the top surface but the bottom is copper colour because of the hairs which turn pale dull colour at maturity.

Flowers are produced in small clusters; both male and female flowers are found. The flower is creamy in colour, and slightly scented. Rounded fruits of 5–7.5 cm in diameter are produced. The colour varies from pink to reddish brown. It is covered with short silky hairs with 4 persistent sepals still attached. As a fruit, it may not be very popular; its flesh is whitish, sweet and quite tasty. It is normally planted from seeds.

Gnemon Tree, Meninjau
Gnetum gnemon
GNETACEAE

Botanically, Meninjau is considered a very primitive plant, probably introduced from Java where it is common. In Peninsular Malaysia it is mainly found in the East Coast. It grows into a tall tree 17–20 metres in height with a nice conical shape canopy. The leaves are 7.5–12.5 cm long by 2.5–7.5 cm wide. They are dark green and shiny above and pale below.

Being a primitive plant more like the pines, male and female cones are produced. These cones are 7.5–12.5 cm long. The female cones do not produce true fruits; the 'fruits' are actually seeds in the botanical sense. Each seed is oblong in shape, smooth in texture, and measuring 2.5–5 cm long and 2 cm wide. It is green when young but turns orange red on ripening. The edible part of the seed *i.e.* skin or rind is bulky. The seeds can be eaten raw or made into biscuits, cakes and savouries.

Indian Jujube, Bedara
Zizyphus mauritiana
RHAMNACEAE

Bedara belongs to a rather uncommon family of thorny plants in Malaysia. It is probably introduced from India. It is a small thorny tree growing up to a height of 10 metres. The thorns arise from the leaf bases. The scented, greenish flowers appear in clusters at the base of the leaf stalks. Fruits are roundish to oblong in

shape, each measuring from 1.8–5 cm long and about 2.5 cm wide. They are green and firm when young, at maturity turning yellow orange to brown. They are eaten raw or as preserved fruits. The flesh is whitish, tastes sourish to sweet. It is like a plum with a stony seed embedded in the flesh.

This fruit is quite common in the northern states of Peninsular Malaysia, growing well in sandy soils. It is propagated from seeds.

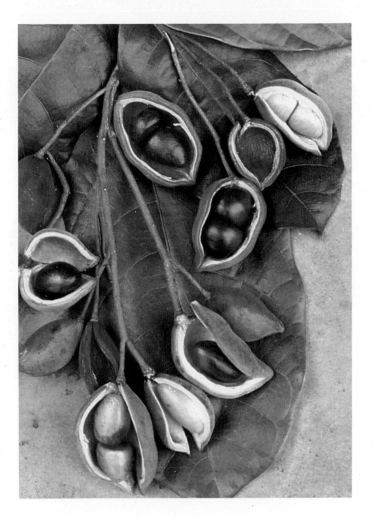

China chestnut, Pheng Phok
Sterculia monosperma
STERCULIACEAE

It is a small tree belonging to the same family as cocoa. The tree is always green and leafy growing to about 10 metres tall. The main stem is short but with many branches. The leaves are large, 12.5–22.5 cm long and 7.5–12.5 cm wide.

Both male and female flowers are reproduced on the same tree. They are pinkish, measuring about 1.2 cm across, and arranged in the form of a panicle at the end of branches. The fruits are in the form of pods, green when unripe, turning to dark red on ripening. They are covered with fine soft hairs, roughly oblong in shape measuring about 7.5–10 cm long and 5 cm wide. The fruit wall is quite thick and the inner wall is pinkish in colour. On splitting, the seeds are visible and they are arranged alternately on the sides of the fruit. Each seed is 2.5–5 cm long and 1.2–2.5 cm wide. The black seeds are shiny and sticky.

This tree is not common in Malaysia except in the state of Perak. The edible seeds can be boiled or roasted. They have a pleasant smell and taste and are consumed mainly by the Chinese.

Ornamental Fruits

Ornamental fruits refer to those that are mainly used as ornamentals or for decorative purposes but may also be edible.

In this chapter, the ornamental fruits described are normally planted for their beauty and brilliance in colour or for their shapes and sizes. They are not grown as fruits for eating and in fact some of these are not edible.

Kumquat, Limau Pagar
Fortunella polyandra
RUTACEAE

Limau Pagar belongs to a group citrus called the Kumquat. It is a known as *Citrus swinglei*, but is now into a separate genus *Fortunella*. Kumq grows well in many tropical a subtropical areas. In Malaysia it is m abundant in Perak and Malacca. T fruits because of their beautiful bri rich yellow colour, are often grown ornamental purpose in addition serving as a drink and preserved frui

Grown in a pot, the plant grows about 1 metre but in the ground, it gro to 3–5 metres tall. Kumquats are sligh different from the citrus group; they thorny but the leaves are long and narr and do not possess the aromatic sm when crushed. The whitish flowers scented, and they appear in a cluster 1–5. The fruits are in the shape of marb of about 2.5 cm in diameter. The text of the skin is smooth, soft and shiny. I green but turning yellow on ripening

Kumquat does well in this country not widely grown. Its cultivation sho be encouraged for its varied use. It can grown from seeds or marcotting. Pot plants are also on sale in the nurserie

Sterculia, Kelumpang
Sterculia foetida

STERCULIACEAE

This is a tall handsome tree from Africa, very useful as an avenue tree. It grows to 10–13 metres with a straight trunk and branches to form a small crown. Various parts of the plants are used, the stem for timber as softwood, seeds for oil and food, leaves for medicinal purposes.

The fruits are green when young, measure about 7.5–10 cm and compressed into the shape of a purse. They turn bright red when ripe, but turning dark with age. The texture is smooth, soft and velvety. When the fruit is ripe, it splits open and the large black seeds can be seen attached alternately on each side. The seeds are edible but not popular or tasty as other species. When eaten in quantities, they have a purgative action and cause headaches. The bright red fruits and trees are therefore mainly used as ornamentals.

Nipple Brinjal, Terong Susu
Solanum mammosum
SOLANACEAE

This species is a semi-woody herb from Central Africa and South America. It grows into a small shrub with large leaves of serrated margin. Thorns or prickles are found on the leaves as well as the stem. The flowers are rather small and insignificant compared to the fruits which are brightly coloured. Fruits are orange in colour, smooth and conical in shape with rounded lobes at its base. They measure about 7.5 cm long and 5 cm across. They also keep well for over a week and when cut can be used for fruit or flower arrangement for indoor decorations. The plant is normally propagated by seeds.

Bottle gourd, Labu, Labu Kendit

Lagenaria leucantha

CUCURBITACEAE

This is a very old cultivated vegetabl at present grown all over the world in tropics and subtropics. The origin probably the Old World around Afri It is a herbaceous plant, usually grown a climber on built pergolas or stak They climb by twinning their stems a also with the aid of tendrils.

The fruit is the attractive part of t plant. The outer layer is hard and tou so that it can be used as a vessel to h water and liquor as it retains the sm and taste. When young, the fruit is gre and soft. The flesh can be eaten as vegetable. The beauty of this fruit also in its shape which enhances its decorat value. It can also be used as a sound b for musical instruments.

Bottle gourd grows easily in any gard soil. Propagation is by means of seeds

rnamental Chilli or pepper,
bai

psicum annum

LANACEAE

In addition to the cooking varieties of
lli or *cabai*, there are many varieties of
llies not normally eaten but are used as
amentals. Ornamental chillies come
various shapes, sizes and colours. They
y be cone, marble, oblong, oval or
rt shaped; bright red, purple creamy,
low, white or green in colour. They are
pagated by seeds, and produce fruit
year round.

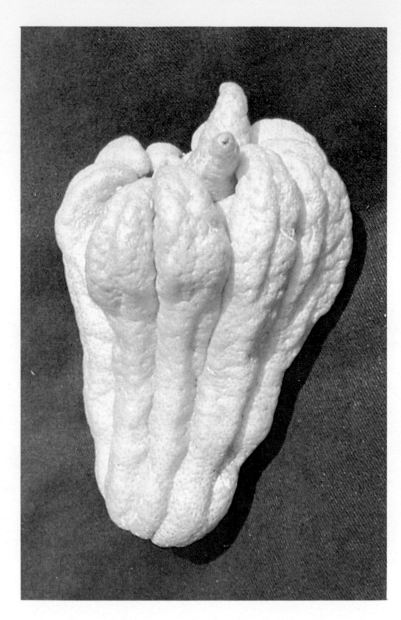

Buddhas' Fingers, Fingered Citron, Limau Sari

Citrus medica
var. *sarcodactylis*

RUTACEAE

This is a variety of the true citr (*Citrus medica*) of the Western world. It) bushy plant growing to a height o metres. In Malaysia, it is found mainly the highlands. The plant is thorny w wingless leaves, a distinguishi character of this species.

The fruits are variable in size, abc 10–17.5 cm long and 5–7.5 cm wi They are green when young but tu yellow on ripening. One end of the frui divided into about 5 parts, ea resembling a finger, hence the na Buddhas' fingers and used for religic purpose. It is also known for its medici value and also serves as an ornamental fruit arrangement.

Wild Fruits

All edible fruits are at one time or another originated from wild fruits many thousands of years ago. Through the process of selection, domestication and breeding, new varieties are produced, which may differ greatly from the original in taste, shape or colour. Through the years many so-called wild fruits have been domesticated, then cultivated on a large scale so that today they become more or less the staple diet of Man. There are many more species in the jungles or forests to be discovered and brought out to be cultivated in the garden or orchard for further investigation. Scientists and explorers all over the world make regular trips to collect and gather these rich natural resources. These new discoveries may one day replace some of the present day fruits.

The wild fruits described in this chapter are edible although not very popular. The wild durian is a good example; it resembles the clonal cultivated ones except that it is smaller, the thorns are thinner and sharper. These so-called wild species found in secondary forests, jungle or wasteland provide the horticultural people with a large pool of plant genetic resources which will be useful in plant breeding.

Soft Fig, Ara Lempong

Ficus obpyramidata

URTICACEAE

This is a wild fig growing widely in Malaysia, occuring in virgin forest especially near water. It is a small tree growing to about 7 metres tall with a upright stem but without a large canop like *Ficus roxburghii*.

The fruits are borne on the stem an branches. They are pear shaped, abou 5–7.5 cm wide, greenish brown in colou when young but turning orangy brow on ripening. They are edible but not ver palatable with a nutty flavour, and th flesh is gummy or sticky. They a attractive as ornamentals but of n economic value. Propagation is by seed

Wild Watermelon,
Timun Dendang

Passiflora foetida

PASSIFLORACEAE

As the botanical name suggests it belongs to the passion fruit family. This species of *Passiflora* originated from Tropical America. Now it grows in parts of the Asian countries as if native. The wild watermelon is a small herbaceous climber, possessing a slender hairy green stem with tendrils. The flowers arise singly but it is quite unique, looking like the passion-fruit flower; the main distinguishing character is the presence of 3 pale green moss-like leaves outside the sepals and they persist even when the fruit is ripe. The fruit is rather small and round, green turning to orange when ripe. It is edible and popular among children in the rural areas as it is found growing in wasteland, by the roadsides and scrambling over grass and bushes. In surburban areas it may be found climbing over fences and hedges.

West Indian Cherry, Buah Ceri
Muntingia calabura
TILIACEAE

Muntingia is not a true cherry; it produces a small round fruit containing many tiny seeds. It is of Mexican origin and introduced into Malaysia only in the 20th century. This leafy small tree of 5–8 metres tall is often grown as a shade tree.

The trees flower all the year round; the flowers are small, creamish in colour. The round fruit measures 1.2 cm in diameter; it is green, but turns pink or red and becomes soft on ripening. It is not tasty but sweet; birds and bats and children go for it.

ᵹ, Ara
us roxburghii
TICACEAE

There are over eighty species of figs in
laysia but most are not edible. The
atability varies enormously, the best
ng the Mediterranean fig *Ficus carica*.
icus roxburghii is one of the edible one

nd locally. It is a relatively short tree
shrub when planted in pots. In the
rden it grows to a height of about 7
etres, with a short trunk and spreading
anches. Fruits of this species are edible
ough not very popular; they can be
ten fresh or made into jam. The figs are
oduced mainly on the trunk but also on
e main branches. They are pear shaped
easuring about 5–10 cm long by 5–7.5
a wide, greenish to brownish in colour
th rough textured skin.
This species should be planted more in
e home garden as shade tree. It grows
ell in deeply cultivated soil and can be
sily propagated by marcots.

Tampoi
Baccaurea griffithii
EUPHORBIACEAE

A large number of Tampoi trees from the Malaysian forest produces good edible fruits. In Sabah, Tampoi Putih (*Baccaurea macrocarpa*) and Tampoi Kuning (*B. puberula*) are as good or even better to eat than the Rambai. The two common jungle species in Peninsular Malaysia are *Baccaurea griffithii* (Greater Tampoi) and *Baccaurea reticulata* (Lesser Tampoi).

Fruits of the Greater Tampoi are large, more or less round and measuring about 2.5–4.0 cm. The skin is dull brownish grey or brownish yellow in colour and slightly rough with little brown spots. The pulp is white and translucent when ripe.

The fruits of the Lesser Tampoi are greyish fawn or brownish buff or yellowish brown. Their pulp is translucent and pale yellow in colour. Its taste is very sweet and pleasant. It is generally regarded as the better of the two species of Tampoi in Peninsular Malaysia.

Morinda, Mengkudu Besar
Morinda citrifolia
RUBIACEAE

Morinda is famous for its dyes in the roots. In India, it is grown as a crop for the dyeing industry; and in Indonesia it is used as a dye in the Batik industry.

Morinda is a small tree or shrub originated from Moluccas. It can grow to a height of 7 metres. It fruits all the year round. The fruits are ellipsoidal in shape, pale yellowish green in colour and shiny. Although attractive, they do not taste good or apetizing, hence not popular.

Pisang Seribu
Wild banana *Musa chiliocarpa*.

Nuts

This group of plants produce true nuts and does not include the coconuts. There are three species found in Malaysia, cashew nut, Brazil nut and the less well known Sapucaia nut. These three species produce seeds which have a hard seed coat, and hence are referred to as nuts. They are hard to crack especially the Brazil nut and Sapucaia nut in which an axe or hammer is required. They are very delicious as well as nutritious.

Cashew nut is produced from a spreading tree growing to 13 metres in height. The fruit is distinctive, being made up of 2 parts *i.e.* a hard nut attached on top of a fleshy fruit. Brazil nut comes from a very tall tree; the nuts are enclosed in a thick fruit, 10–15 cm wide. The nuts of the Sapucaia tree is of the same nature as the Brazil nut. Brazil nut as the name suggests is a native of the Brazilian forest. Although they are not planted as crops in the wild state they are collected for export. In Malaysia they are also not common. The nuts are very popular throughout the world, being used in confectionary and as nuts.

Cashew nut is better known in Malaysia than the others, although it is not a common tree in gardens or backyards. They are grown in commercial scale in sandy soils of the East Coast of Peninsular Malaysia. It can be a potential crop for the export market.

azil Nut

rtholletia excelsa

CYTHIDACEAE

Brazil nut is a native of the Amazon
est in South America, found wild in the
est and not as a cultivated crop. The
e is very tall, growing up to 33 metres
h with a small crown. Mature leaves
dark green turning to brownish red at
escence. Long panicles of flowers are
oduced, the flowers are about 2.5 cm
de. The fruits are attached to a thick
lk. They are large and hard, measuring
–15 cm wide and 15–20 cm long, dark
own in colour with a rough surface. At
tip of the fruit is a lid-like structure,
ich on ripening falls off and the seeds
through this opening. Each fruit may
ntain 10–15 nuts which are closely
cked. Each nut is 3.7–6.2 cm long,
angular in cross section. The coat is
gh, rough and brown in colour. The
ble part of the nut is the creamish
ite kernel inside each nut.

Brazil nut is not a commercial crop
ither is it seen around much in
alaysia. It was first planted in the early
oo. At present these specimens are
nd in Serdang Crop Production

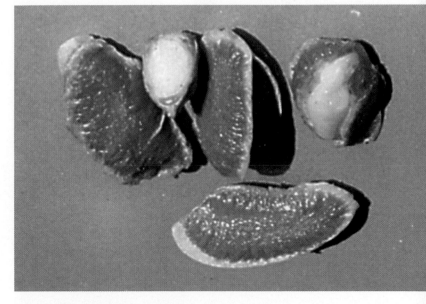

Centre. They come to production 8–10
years after planting. They are self sterile,
therefore groups of plants have to be
planted together as single tree does not
produce fruits. The fruits take over a year
to ripen.

Sapucaia Nut
Lecythis ollaria,
LECYTHIDACEAE

This tree is less well known a
popular than the cashew or Brazil nut.
origin is also South America, in the fo
of Brazil. It is also grown in a wild st
but not as a crop, hence seeds
collected by hand and is not easy du
the size of tree and the population
scattered all over the forest.

In cultivation it is a handsome t
with a large spreading crown. It is m
branched and grows to a height of
metres. The tree shows sign of winter
at certain times of the year.

The sapucaia nuts come i
production about 10 years after planti
Large fruits are produced from the tip
the branches; they are so heavy that
branches droop. They measure fr
7.5–25 cm across, conical in shape a
with a ridge at the base. At maturity
lid opens and the seeds fall off. The fru
very woody and hard, rough and bro
in colour. In each fruit, the number
seeds varies from 10–30. The nuts (see
although not as popular, have a pleas
taste, rich in oil similar to the Brazil n

Sapucaia nuts are grown in Serda
The seeds take a long time to germina
and grow very slowly to maturity.

Cashew nut, Gajus

Anarcardium occidentale

ANACARDIACEAE

This is one of the most popular nuts of tropical origin. In Malaysia, it is grown in sandy soils mainly in the East Coast.

Cashew nut is a small spreading tree reaching to a height of up to 13 metres. The main stem is stout and short. The young leaves are edible.

The cashew nut flowers, measuring about 1.2 cm across, appear normally after a spell of dry weather, with several flowering periods per year. The flowers are produced in bunches as a panicle, producing a scent.

It takes about 4 years for trees grown from seed to bear fruit. The fleshy fruit is made up of 2 parts, about 7.5–10 cm long at the tip of which is a hard curved nut of commercial value. The nut must be heated (boiling or roasting) to destroy a poison which is an irritant. Plants can be propagated by seeds or by budding.

Highland Fruits

Many temperate fruit species have been introduced into this country, a few survived and manage to grow only in the highlands of altitude over 1000 metres where the temperature is much lower than the lowlands. Under lowland conditions the temperate species fail miserably. Even at the highlands, in the absence of a cold chill and suitable daylength, many species fail to flower and set seeds.

A few temperate fruits such as strawberries, raspberries, mulberries, tree tomato and various citrus, grow in the hill resorts such as Cameron Highlands, Maxwell Hill, Genting Highlands and Fraser's Hill. Vegetable species of temperate origin are, however, more plentiful. Some of the temperate species become adapted to tropical lowland conditions but they do not perform as well as in the cool climate. The beautiful strawberries we see in the supermarkets are imported; the local highland fruits do not attain their maximum size and brilliance in colour.

Strawberry
Fragaria vesca
ROSACEAE

The strawberry, the most popular and common of the berries in temperate countries, is quite an easy small plant to grow. It has a creeping habit, producing creeping stems or runners on the ground. It is slow growing, forming mounds up to 15–20 cm high. The flowers are white with gold coloured centres from which

berries are formed. The fruit is a compound one made up of tiny fruitlets. It is green at first, turning to bright shiny red as it ripens. It is delightfully scented and is eaten fresh or made into jam.

In the highlands, strawberries are useful for the home garden; they need little space and fruit continuously. New plants can be propagated from the mother plant by cutting off from the rooted runners. They grow well in well-drained soil.

93

Sweet Orange, Jaffa Orange, Limau Manis, Chula, Choreng
Citrus sinensis
RUTACEAE

The sweet orange is the type normally imported from western countries in the temperate zones, hence it is grown and doing well in the Cameron Highlands where the temperature is more favourable than the lowlands. It differs from the other local sweet oranges in that the skin does not peel off easily like the mandarin or the local sweet orange. Another characteristic is the vertical streaks on the skin of the fruit.

The sweet orange plant is a woody shrub which grows to a height of about 5 metres. The leaf measures about 10–12.5 cm by 2.5–3.75 cm. The top surface is dark green and the bottom paler green. There is no distinct wing on the petiole. It is oblong in shape, tapering at both ends but the tip is not pointed while the margins are slightly indented.

The fruit is round, measuring about 10 cm in diameter. It is green when young, turning to yellowish green and finally orange in colour. The skin is fairly rough but quite .thin, about 25–30 mm, enclosing about 12 segments which are seeded. The flesh varies from yellow to orange in colour. It is very juicy and sweet and not fibrous.

The cultivation of this species should be encouraged, as it is doing very well in the highlands. It can be easily propagated from seeds or by marcotting.

Mulberry, Tut, Besaram
Morus alba
URTICACEAE

The mulberry is a small tree or bush spreading from the highlands of Himalaya to China. It does not thrive as well in the lowlands but fruits well at higher altitudes.

Mulberries are mainly planted for their leaves to feed the silkworms. Their fruits are, however, edible but not very tasty, hence not popular and not available in the market. They are rather small compared to strawberries, measuring about 4 cm long by 1.25 cm in diameter. The colour changes from light pinkish red to bright dark red on ripening.

Tree Tomato
Cyphomandra betacea
SOLANACEAE

The tree tomato is a food crop, native to the highlands of South America, but now spreading to Sri Lanka, India and the East. At high elevations it grows to around 3 metres high. It is a shrub or a small tree with a spreading crown and short trunk. The leaves are fairly large, 15–20 cm long by 12.5 cm wide, and are cordate in shape with a pointed tip.

The flowers, appearing in groups of 3–4 or in clusters, are pinkish in colour and measure about 2.5 cm across. They produce a nice scent. The fruits are oblong in shape and measure 5 cm long.

The colour is pale green, turning yellow to bright red on ripening. The egg-shaped, smooth fruits are produced throughout the year. They are eaten raw, being succulent and slightly acidic, cooked for food as a stew, or made into jam.

Tree tomato grows best in well-irrigated loamy soil. Plants are commonly propagated by means of seeds which germinate readily. This plant is useful as a garden plant to substitute for tomatoes.

Fruit Arrangement

Many fruits are as beautiful, colourful and bright as the flowers and undoubtedly will be useful resources for decorative purposes similar to that of flower arrangement. Fruits indeed can provide endless scope for imaginative use in decorative arrangement.

Fruit arrangement in a way must have originated long ago in the great feasts for kings and queens. It is not as popular as flower arrangement because to the majority of people it will be considered a waste to place fruits in a manner to feast the eyes and not for consumption. Nowadays, in the more affluent society, fruit arrangement is coming into the scene. Indeed fruits are useful raw materials for the interior decorators as well as the housewife.

Fruit arrangement is not a well developed art as Ikebana where there are fixed principles taught in various schools. Nonetheless, nowadays there are professionals in fruit arrangement, mainly at flower shows or exhibitions and also for exclusive dinners in large hotels.

However, to the ordinary people with limited resources, we can attempt in a simple way to lay down our fruits on the dining table in a more attractive manner. Fruits can be arranged according to individual taste as beauty mainly lies in the eyes of the beholder. In this chapter we are not describing the principles and methods of fruit arrangement but rather

The following is a list of fruits described in this book which are suitable for various types of arrangement described in this chapter.

1. *Fresh fruit arrangement:* Starfruit, Oranges, Lemons, Jambu, Mangosteen, Pulasan, Rambutan, Decorative Brinjals and Gourds, Pineapple.

to introduce the resources that are available and how they can be used in fruit arrangement.

The scope for fruit arrangement is endless. It is left to our own imagination. Basically fruit arrangement for the sake of convenience can be grouped into three categories, the fresh-fruit arrangement, dry arrangement, and the cut- or carved-fruit arrangement.

2. *Dry arrangement:* Sterculia, Gourds, Brazil nut, Sapucaia nut, Pomegranate, Coconut, Jering hutan.
3. *Cut- or carved-fruit arrangement:* Watermelon, Pomelo, Papaya, Starfruit, Pineapple, Coconut, Fruit vegetables.

In exhibitions and flower shows, fruit arrangement has to be in a fairly big scale to make an impact. For the centre piece,

an arrangement may be as large as 2 metres tall and 3 metres wide, in the shape of a large crown, a giant hamper, a crest, a mural, or any words representing a motto or design. Each arrangement may be composed with small colourful fruits, such as jambu, rambutan, pulasan

and decorative brinjal, using a large number of each type to provide the necessary colours, or if large fruits such as coconut, pineapple, pomelo are used, a smaller number of each type would be required.

In a small scale, a collection of fresh fruits can be attractively arranged at home with the aid of some of the local-made containers like pewter fruit bowl, mengkuang baskets, rotan baskets or trays, or porcelain and clay plates.

Dry arrangement is another area of fruit arrangement for those who are not so energetic as they need not change their arrangement too regularly; this can last for months or years. A few fruits at maturity become dry naturally; these are the nuts like Sapucaia and Brazil nuts. Others such as gourds, pomegranate, capsicum and lemons can be dried artificially to preserve the fruits in their natural state.

The Sapucaia and Brazil nuts are very large and can be kept forever as they are very hard and woody. They can be made into decorative ash trays as well as

containers for dry flowers. Gourds in particular are grown for fruit and flower arrangement. Because of their various shapes and colours they are very useful for both fresh and dry arrangement. After drying, gourds can be varnished with a spray of polyurethane or even with hair lacquer to give a shiny effect. These shapely gourds arranged on a tray, in a copper pan, or a large wooden bowl make a beautiful decoration in the flat, house or office. The gourds may lose their natural colour in time; in such cases they can be painted or stained with shoe polish, or they can be bleached, later painted or carved. Dry gourds are very light and can be used as mobiles or wall collages.

Finally fruits can be cut or carved to enhance their beauty before being eaten. Many fruits are normally served cut as they are too big, for example the pineapple, watermelon, papaya, starfruit and many others. These fruits can be cut at different angles to bring out the best effect of shape and size, for example starfruit when cut transversely will produce pieces of stars which can be arranged beautifully and effectively on a plate to make it more attractive. In addition, one can also cut or carve the fruits into various shapes or into different types of natural containers. One good example is carving and cutting the watermelon into the shape of a basket with a handle and inside it, one can put fruit salad for serving. Another possibility is with a large pineapple which can be cut into two longitudinal halves, the content scooped off and other fruit cocktail put in its place.

In the case of large fruits with soft and easily cut skin such as the pomelo, it is possible to remove the green or yellow skin and carve flowers and animals on them. There is no end for such creations. It is left to one's ingenuity and imagination to present something more attractive and novel at the dinner table.

Brinjal or Egg Plant *Solanum melongena*

Some Useful Fruits for Arrangement

Pithecellobium ellipticum.

Solanum sp.

Pumpkin (*Cucurbita moschata*).

...ulia foetida.

Sterculia parvifolia.

Wax gourd (*Benincasa cerifera*).

Sterculia foetida.

Egg Plant *Solanum melongena*.

Cherry Tomato *Lycopersicon esculentum*.

Tomatoes—*Lycopersicon esculentum.*

Seasonality
of Fruits

Why my fruit trees do not bear fruits? This is a very common question asked by home gardeners and farmers. The answers to this are both very numerous and variable, ranging from fairy tale types to very scientific ones. In order to appreciate this problem, one should try to understand the structure and biology of flowers, in particular the reproductive physiology.

Plants produce flowers and they can be of three types—male, female and hermaphrodite (mixed sexes or bisexual). In some cases a plant produces either only male or female flowers, some produce both sexes in the same plant, and finally

Female papaya plant.

those that produce bisexual flowers. One good example is the papaya which can be of three different types. A plant can be a male, that is only male flowers are produced, and therefore will not normally bear any fruit. Whereas it can also be a female or a hermaphrodite plant which will produce female and bisexual flowers respectively hence they will bear fruits. Therefore, the sexes of the plants will basically determine whether plants will produce fruits or not.

With the potential ability to reproduce, that is the right sex, they may still not set fruit or in extreme cases, may not even produce flowers. There are many factors which control and affect the flowering habits of plants. These factors include pollination, fertilization, nutrition of trees, water, light and in fact the environment as a whole. In this chapter an attempt will be given to explain why trees do not flower under certain conditions and how to induce flowering.

In temperate countries with four definite seasons (summer, autumn, winter and spring), plants have definite pattern of growth and development. In winter, the conditions are not favourable for growth as the temperature will be too low. When spring comes it is the time for new planting, and old trees will produce new flushes of green leaves, then flower and followed by fruiting. With some species, there are new outbursts of flower blossoms without leaves, for example the Cherry Blossom. In Autumn, the leaves senesce and fall, followed by a period of rest in winter. So the life cycle goes on year after year.

In the tropics the weather is normally

Male papaya plant.

favourable for growth all the year round except during drought. In spite of this, plants may not even flower once a year; there are cases of some species flowering once in seven years. Generally speaking, most seasonal fruits flower once or twice a year, for example Durian, Rambutan, Mangosteen, Langsat, Duku, *etc*. Many local fruits are, however, non seasonal; they flower and produce fruits all the year round for example, Papaya, Guava, Custard Apple, Nangka, Citrus, *etc*.

The seasonal fruits depend on weather conditions for flowering; in particular they require a dry spell to induce flowering. In this country seasonal fruits appear in the market about twice a year, around the middle and end of the year. Usually an alternating season or year of prolific fruiting is the pattern. This is particularly true for Durian whereas Rambutan responds less to dry weather so that there is more frequent and regular fruiting.

Most of the fruit trees are perennials; they flower and fruit for a number of years. Many do not flower until they are mature; the period of pure vegetative growth may vary from 3 to 12 years. This is particularly true for those plants grown from seeds which will take longer time to flower in contrast to budgrafted and marcotted plants. One should therefore

Mango in fruit.

know the source of the planting material before complaining why some taller or older plants do not flower while the neighbour's fruit trees flower faster and within a short period of planting.

Besides the weather or environmental conditions and source of planting materials many other cultural practices, chemical and biotic factors greatly influence flowering.

The seasonal perennial fruit trees bear

ngo in vegetative stage *i.e.* off season.

New flush of growth in Sapucaia nut tree.

fertilizer are made up of nitrogen, phosphorus or phosphate, and potassium or potash. Nitrogen contributes towards vegetative growth and phosphate affects flowering. In a fertilizer application programme, young seedlings or plants can be given higher dosage of nitrogen for faster growth whereas at the later stages, *i.e.* reproductive stage, more phosphate should be given to promote flowering. There is a wide range of fertilizers available in the market, in which the composition has been adjusted for various purposes to cater for different species of fruit trees and flowering plants. Very often there are cases of over fertilization which may kill the plant or induce prolific vegetative growth only, hence you get a very nice healthy tree with lots of dark green leaves and not a single fruit. The obvious solution of this problem is to stop fertilizer application but provide more phosphate to the plant. Another alternative is to prune off excess foliage. Some old folks may advise one to slash the trunk or bang a number of nails on the stem to induce flowering and fruiting.

their flowers on different parts of the tree, some on the trunk itself (e.g. Namnam), on the main stem and branches (e.g. Blimbing Asam), and lastly on new shoots and twigs of trees (e.g. Rambutan). The fruiting habit of trees will determine whether pruning is necessary or not after each fruiting season. For example, those that produce flowers and fruits only from new shoots or twigs have to be pruned after each season so as to induce production of new shoots, and consequently there will be more flowering and fruiting sites, hence a more prolific fruit season. Whereas pruning is not so important in the annual fruit trees and those that produce fruits on the trunk and mature branches.

An understanding of plant nutrition is useful. The main constituents of any

Recently with further advancement in reproductive physiology, the use of plant hormones has been introduced. This kind of hormone treatment can be encouraged. Indeed with pineapple this has been practised for a long time using either ethylene or naphthyl acetic acid to induce even flowering so that the fruits can be harvested at the same time. Plant hormones can be used not only to induce flowering but also for fruit set, increase fruit size, *etc.*

Having induced flowering in fruit trees is not enough. The trees may produce many blossoms and yet not a single fruit. The reasons for this are many. There may be the absence of insects or other pollinating agents in which case the flowers will not be pollinated and fertilized to set fruit. Normally there are sufficient insects, such as bees, moths and ants to pollinate the flowers. If they are lacking, bees may be introduced or other means of assisted pollination have to be carried out. Besides insects, bats are also pollinating agents for Durian and other flowers. Even successful pollination and fertilization will not ensure a prolific crop. By nature, not all fruits will remain intact; some will fall so that there is enough room for the remaining fruits to grow. Many pests and diseases affect the fruits especially when they are young.

Hence they have to be protected by bagging, for example in Starfruit and Nangka. An alternative is to spray them with chemical protectants. One can also add foliar fertilizers and spray them against diseases and pests. One successful treatment has been demonstrated with mangoes, in which regular fortnightly sprays of a combination of insecticides and fertilizer promote better fruit set. A mixture of Wellgrow fertilizer Manzeb D and Bidrin has been used successfully.

Wintering in Sapucaia nut tree.

The Mango in full bloom

Propagation, Planting and Maintenance

Propagation, planting and maintenance of plants are the key to success in producing high quality fruits. Gardeners must be aware that fruit trees raised from seeds may not grow true to type like their parents. Hence vegetative propagation by budding and marcotting is practised whenever possible. Planting a fruit tree correctly is equally important, for example planting in the right site, soil and manner will ensure it to grow to its full potential. Lastly even with the best planting material and correctly planted, fruit trees cannot be productive without proper maintenance—pruning, watering, manuring and protecting them from pests, diseases and weeds.

Failure to observe these three important stages in fruit production will undoubtedly result in poor yield as judged by the fruits during harvest. A plant with even the lowest standard of maintenance will survive, but it may not bear fruits, and even if fruits are borne, they will be small, diseased, or pest infested which are not fit for eating. On

Seedlings in seed box.

while some reproduce by asexual means or vegetatively. In the latter the plants have the ability to produce adventitious roots from various parts of the plant, which when they become detached from the mother plant will grow into independent new plants, thus reproducing themselves vegetatively. Man through this observation has improvised and developed many techniques such as leaf, root and stem cuttings, grafting, budding, inarching, marcotting and the latest method is tissue culture. In tissue culture a small piece of tissue when macerated is capable of producing thousands of identical plants. This technique is still new and used only in well established organizations. Therefore in this chapter only the common methods of propagation within the reach of the home gardeners will be described.

SEEDS

Seeds are the main source of planting material; even if vegetative propagation such as budgrafting is practised one still needs a seedling root stock. Seeds are obtained from ripe, mature fruits. They are washed and cleaned before planting. Some seeds such as Rambutan, Durian and Citrus cannot be dried before sowing, as they die on drying; these are the recalcitrant seeds. Seeds are normally sown in seed boxes or pots. When the seedlings are 5–7.5 cm tall they are

the other hand, a selected plant of a well known clone, planted in the correct manner and well maintained will bear fruits which will bring you joy and pride.

In this chapter, the basic information on propagation, planting and maintenance will be described to serve as a guide in your gardening. Only some of the basic principles are dealt with. As there are a tremendous number of species and varieties of fruits found locally, it is almost impossible that a particular recommendation be applicable to all the different crops. In general, if all the principles discussed are observed, one can be rest assured that reasonable quality fruits will be produced for consumption or sale.

PLANT PROPAGATION

In nature, most flowering plants reproduce sexually by means of seeds

Seedlings in poly bags.

transplanted into plastic bags to undergo a process of hardening *i.e.* exposed to more harsh conditions as out in the open. When seedlings are about 20–25 cm tall they can be planted in the field. Larger seeds such as Durian and Rambutan, are normally sown in shaded seed beds or directly in large polythene bags in the nursery. These are the two main ways whereby seedlings are produced for planting a crop either as a true seedling or as a seedling root stock for budding or grafting.

MARCOTTING

Marcotting or air layering is a form of vegetative propagation. New individuals are obtained from the parent plant. The limitation is that not many plants can be obtained from the parent plant and the resultant parent plant will be out of shape when many of the branches are removed as marcots. The advantage of this technique is that you can get a plant which will bear fruits immediately when it is planted.

The technique is simple. Select a good desirable clone as a parent plant as the new plants obtained will yield the same type of fruits as the parent. Choose from the branches a vigorous growing shoot

A selected shoot for marcotting.

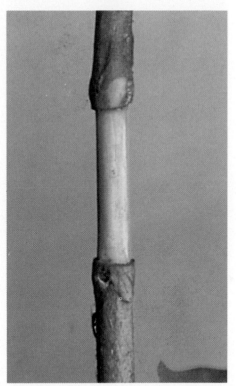

Bark removed from shoot.

about the size of a pencil. With a sharp budding knife make two complete cuts round the circumference of the shoot, the distance between the cuts being about twice the diameter of the shoot. The bark

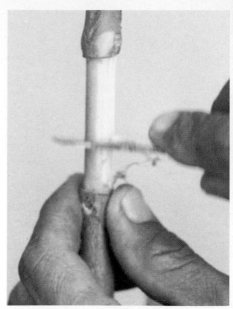

between the two cuts is completely removed, the exposed part of the wood is scraped with the knife to remove the cambium. Meanwhile a rooting medium consisting of clay and cowdung moistened

Cambium is scraped off.

Soil mixture is placed over scraped wood.

The ball of soil mixture is wrapped in plastic sheet and tied at both ends.

A rooted marcot is ready to be cut off.

with water is prepared. Make the mixture into the shape of a ball in your hand, then flatten it, place it under the cut wood and plaster the mixture round the cut wood again to make it into a ball shape. Place a piece of polythene sheet (37 × 30 cm) below, wrap it round the ball of mixture, and tie both ends to enclose the ball of earth. After 6–8 weeks, examine the marcot and see whether roots have developed or not. When the marcot has sufficient roots it can be removed by cutting it off from the parent plant, and a new plant is produced. This can be planted in a pot followed by field planting.

117

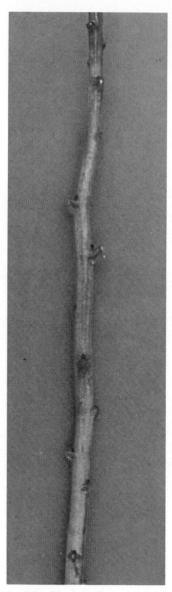

A stick of budwood.

BUDGRAFTING

For plants that do not root readily, another form of vegetative propagation commonly used is budgrafting, although there are other types of grafts involving the union of different parts of plants together.

As the name suggests, it involves the union of a bud together with a seedling rootstock. A good quality clone is first selected for propagation. The buds of that particular clone for propagation are selected and obtained as budwood, from which a number of buds can be obtained.

The other essential part is the seedling rootstocks which can be of any clone as long as they are of the same species, for example Rambutan R4 can be grafted on to Rambutan seedlings of any clone. Seedlings are obtained from nursery beds or in large polythene bags. The seedlings are to be of reasonable size, about 1.2–1.8 cm in diameter. Once both the budwood

Bud is lifted from the wood.

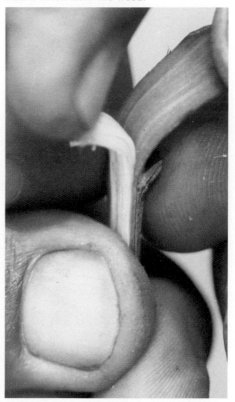

A bud is removed from budwood.

and seedling rootstock are ready, one can carry out the grafting.

Budwood is normally obtained from the budwood nursery of a selected clone. A piece of budwood about 30 cm long is cut; this budwood will yield about 4–5 buds. With a budding knife make a deep cut about 5–7.5 cm long with the knife entering the wood about 1–1.2 cm above

The bud is tied to the stock.

a bud and the cut finishes about 1.2 cm below the bud. The piece of bud is lifted up and the piece of wood from the central part of the bud is detached gently from the green bark. Trim off the ends of the bud so that it is about rectangular in shape measuring 3.0 cm by 0.6 cm. The bud is then ready for grafting onto the stock.

The seedling rootstock is to receive the bud. A horizontal cut is made at a distance about 15–25 cm from the ground level. Then a vertical cut is made at the centre to form an inverted T. With the sharp budding knife lift up the bark along the vertical slit. The prepared bud can now be inserted between the raised bark flaps of the seedling stock. The bud is then pushed gently into the inverted T and the flaps of the bark are closed over it, exposing only the bud. The preparation and insertion should be done rapidly to prevent the tissue from drying or else the percentage success will be low. Tie the bud firmly with raffia or plastic tape so that the bud is in good contact with the cambium of the seedling. Several turns of the tape are made round the stem except for a very small portion of the bud, and in some cases a leaf is tied over the bud so as

Bud is inserted in the stock.

to prevent excessive exposure to heavy rain and sunlight.

After about a fortnight the bud can be examined by loosening the tape. If the bud is still green this means the budding is successful. One may find the bud sprouting, in which case the stock is cut off at a point 2.5–5 cm above the point of insertion of the bud. This is to enable the new bud to grow vigorously. To be less drastic part of the shoot can be retained till the new bud has grown to 5–7 cm in length. Thereafter any new shoots coming out from the seedling rootstock have to be removed, so as not to interfere with the growth of the new bud and this will also ensure fruits from this budgrafted plant will be true to type and not bearing fruits from the seedling stock of unknown quality.

New shoot from bud graft.

PLANTING

Planting is best carried out at the beginning of the rainy season as the root system can develop before the dry season and ensure better establishment. In a small garden, one or two plants can be planted even in the dry weather, provided there is regular watering. Nowadays most fruit trees are planted as budgrafted, grafted or marcotted plants in pots or large plastic bags and seedlings too are often in plastic bags before field planting. This is a convenient method; the plants receive better attention when they are in the nursery, but once they are planted in the field it is not physically possible to water plants over a few hundred acres. Whether trees are established from seeds or vegetative means such as budding, grafting and marcotting, they have to be planted correctly for optimum fruit production.

Before planting, a suitable site must be selected in areas with good soil and drainage. Having chosen the site, planting holes have to be prepared to receive the plants. In most areas the ground of the garden is made up of subsoil especially in housing estates. Therefore fairly large planting holes with replacement of good soil i.e. burnt earth or compost with cowdung is necessary. The average planting hole should be about 1 m × 1 m by 1 m deep. Smaller hole is, however acceptable provided the soil is not lateritic or clayey.

A square is marked out on the ground. On digging the soil from the top half of

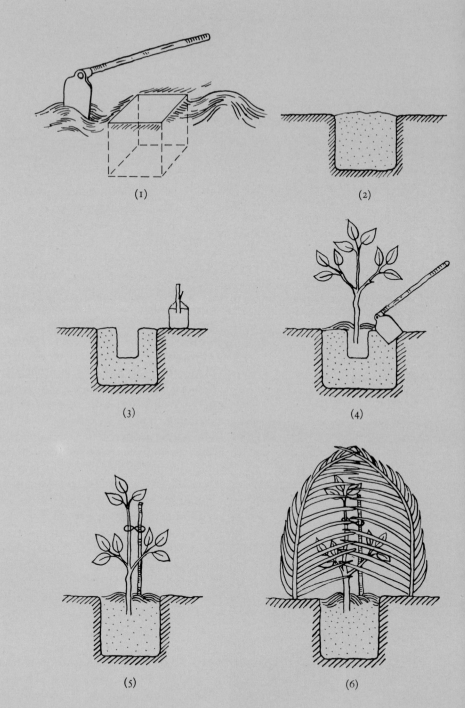

Figure 1. Stages in planting seedlings or grafted plant:
    (1) A planting hole is dug.
    (2) Hole is filled with soil mixture.
    (3) Small hole is dug in the planting area.
    (4) Seedling is lowered into hole.
    (5) Seedling is tied to a stake.
    (6) Seedling is shaded.

the hole can be kept on one side and the bottom half or subsoil on the other. Wherever possible replace the entire soil with burnt earth, compost and organic matter such as cow or chicken dung. If this is not possible then make use of the soil from the top half of the hole and mixed it with topsoil from other part of the garden and add organic manure or compost together with about 500 grams of complete fertilizer. Filled the hole with the soil mixture, water a few times and allow soil to settle down before planting.

When the planting hole is ready to receive the plant, the plant is carefully removed from its container, usually just by slitting the plastic bag and carefully take out the plant with the root system intact. With the cangkol dig a small hole in the centre of the planting hole, the size about that of the container in which the plant is taken out. Place the plant into the small hole and fill it with soil so that its level is the same as the planting hole. Make sure the new plant stays firmly in the soil by compressing the soil around the plant. The surface of the soil is then levelled and a layer of mulch or dried decayed leaves or compost is used to cover the soil. Water the plant after planting. If the plant is weak, a stake can be put into the soil and the plant is tied to the stake. It is also advisable to provide some shade initially. From now on the work of the gardener is mainly on maintenance of the trees.

MAINTENANCE

WATERING OR IRRIGATION

Water is essential for life. All plants require a regular supply of water either naturally from rain or artificially from a watering can. Plants will respond to watering, the amount of which depends on the stage of growth, the type of soil and the climate. A young tree newly transplanted will require regular watering whereas a more mature tree over 3 years old with its deeper root system can get sufficient water at the deeper levels of the soil. A sandy soil will also require more water. Whenever possible a newly planted tree should be given water twice a day, once in the morning and another in the evening. Insufficient water will lead to wilting of the plant and may result in death. When watering seedlings in seed beds or in small plastic bags, use a hose attached to the watering can to prevent washing away both the seed and soil. One way of preventing water loss is by using a mulch over the soil around the plant. Another way is to scoop the soil around the base of the plant to form a ridge and a basin around the plant; this will ensure that water applied is not run off but absorbed mostly by the roots.

With large areas of orchards it is not economical to do hand watering, an irrigation system has to be introduced. A pump is necessary to pump water into a storage tank and then distributed by a network of hose or pipes. Furrow irrigation is another way of watering fruit trees in an orchard.

FERTILIZERS

Besides water a plant needs other nutrients for growth and fruit production. A combination of various elements is required. Those in sulphate of ammonia, superphosphate, and sulphate of potash are the three main sources of NPK fertilizers since they supply the essential elements nitrogen (N) phosphate (P) and potash (K). There are other elements required in smaller amounts such as magnesium, zinc and boron. These are usually included in a complete fertilizer. If a plant has insufficient nutrients it will show signs of weak growth and yellowing of leaves; other symptoms include the die back of leaves and there may be other colorations on the leaves. This will lead to severe reduction in crop yield.

Nutrients may be applied as organic manures in the form of cowdung, chicken dung and compost. They not only supply nutrients but also improve the soil structure. Hence organic fertilizers is much preferred. The caution to note is, to apply only well rotted organic manure and do not use fresh manure from the animals.

A combination of manure and fertilizers is the best. Fertilizers are usually in the form of either powder or as granules. Nowadays fertilizers are granulated from a complete mixture of elements required by the trees. A general fertilizer would have NPK in the ratio of 15:15:15 but many combinations are available depending on the type of trees to be applied, for example a citrus tree if given a very high application of nitrogen will produce a lot of large leaves and develop a weak stem and branches and the yield and quality of fruits will be poor. One should not apply excessive fertilizers — the general rule is to apply little and often.

The amount and frequency of fertilizer application depends on the state of growth of the trees and also on the type of soil and climate. A small seedling needs less fertilizer. If the soil is poor there is greater need and one should not apply fertilizer on dry season as it may damage the roots.

The standard of maintenance varies, the home gardeners may spend much more time and effort as compared to large orchards of a few hundred acres. With home gardeners, fertilizers should be applied just below the leaf canopy where most of the feeder roots are located. With the help of a changkol or rake remove the weeds, broadcast the fertilizer around the trunk, at least 30 cm from the main stem.

Raking in fertilizer.

The fertilizer is then raked into the soil surface. The frequency of application is at least 4 times a year. Both organic farm manure and fertilizers can be applied at the same time. Some of the organic fertilizers are long lasting, releasing the nutrients very slowly over a long period.

FOLIAR FERTILIZATION

It is a well known fact that leaves can absorb nutrients. This fact is of particular value in foliar fertilization. In cases where there is difficulty in absorption of nutrients through the roots or there is an urgent need due to deficiency, foliar application can bring about faster response as nutrients can get in direct to the plant and not through the soil.

Foliar fertilizer can be either complete *i.e.* containing all the essential and trace elements or it can just contain the element that is deficient. On the whole a complete formulation is used as it is difficult to detect the exact element that is lacking. Foliar fertilizer comes in the market as a liquid or solid; the solid formulations are 100% soluble in water.

Foliar fertilizer may be applied on its own, or mixed with pesticides and apply together which will save a lot of labour. The mixture can be applied with an ordinary hand sprayer, directing the solution on the leaves as a fine mist. The amount to be applied is always given in the directions of the various brands of foliar fertilizers.

DISEASE AND PEST CONTROL

In the tropics with the high humidity and temperature, fungi and insects thrive very well. As a result many of the fruit trees suffer from attack of diseases and from pests.

As prevention is better than cure, one should try to keep the garden clean by burning all dead parts of plant. Any new introduction into the garden should be sprayed for pests and common diseases. For precaution, a general copper fungicide should be given once every 3–4 weeks during wet season and reduced to once every 6–8 weeks in dry weather. Make regular inspection of the leaves and fruits and look out for spots on leaves and fruits, curling of leaves, deformed fruits and dieback of shoots. Try to identify diseases before applying the spray.

Many insects bite, suck and eat the leaves, fruits and roots of fruit trees. Like diseases, one must identify the types of insects and their feeding habits before an efficient spraying can be applied. Pesticides are in the form of liquid and powder for which a small hand sprayer can be effective. Dusting and spraying at regular intervals (once every 4–6 weeks) is a preventive measure. The directions for use of these chemicals are given in the containers of fungicides and pesticides. The common pests of fruit trees are scale insects, aphids, red spiders, mealy bugs, grasshoppers, leaf-eating beetles and caterpillars. White ants can also damage fruit trees by attacking the roots and bark of trees.

WEED CONTROL

A weed is defined commonly as a plant in the wrong place. Weeds compete with the crop for water and fertilizers and also can host disease organisms and pests, as such they are undesirable and have to be controlled. Weeds are particularly bad for the crop plant especially at the young stage of growth. Special care must be given to get rid of them around the crop plants.

Weeds are at their worst during the rainy season. They grow very rapidly and may even smother the crop plant. Therefore it is best to remove the weeds while they are still young. Weeding is usually carried out manually in a small scale especially for home gardeners, with the help of a changkol, rake or hoe. They may also be controlled by spraying a weedicide which will kill the weeds but not the crop plant.

In weeding seedlings, if possible remove all weeds in the seedbed, pots, or plastic bags. Once the tree is mature ring weeding is practised i.e. remove all the weeds round the main stem below the leaf canopy.

Weeding.

With all the watering, fertilizers application, protection from pests and weeds, fruit trees may still not produce fruits at their maximum potential if proper pruning is not carried out at various stages of plant growth. Pruning is a process whereby part of a tree is removed to induce growth of certain parts, to remove diseased and dead parts, to create more fruiting branches, or to give the tree a better shape.

The shape and size of trees can be controlled by pruning. Pruning for shape is carried out when the trees are still young *i.e.* just planted at their permanent site in the garden. The main objective is to produce a tree with a straight main trunk with no branches for a distance of 1–2 metres from the ground level. The branches should arise from the upper part of the trunk to form a rounded shape canopy. This will enable easier weeding, fertilizer application and even harvesting.

Allow the main shoot to grow straight with the help of a stake. In the case of bud-grafted plants make sure all shoots from the old seedling rootstock are removed so that only the budded variety is allowed to grow vigorously. This type of pruning at the early stage to shape the tree is called formative pruning and this will determine the final shape of the tree when it matures.

Once the plant has grown to maturity and in fact throughout its life all diseased and broken branches are to be pruned by sawing in a downward direction. The cut ends of the branches should be trimmed and painted with tar to prevent rotting.

There are a number of trees which flower on the new shoots, for example, the Rambutan. The flowers and fruits are found at the end of the shoots. If these are pruned off after each fruiting season, the plant will not only look better but there are more new shoots formed and certainly there will be more fruits in the next season. When pruning fruit trees, removal of some shoots will provide better air circulation and penetration of light which will help to ripen the wood before bud formation.

Besides shoots, branches and leaves, roots may also be pruned. The practice is to cut a trench about a metre deep round the tree and about 1–3 metres from the trunk depending on the size of the tree. Root pruning is to check over luxurious growth of the foliage in order to promote flowering. Another reason of root pruning is to minimize the shock of transplanting; root pruning is usually carried out a week or two before transplanting of the whole tree.

Index to Common Names

Index to Botanical Names